THE ALTERNATIVE TO NUCLEAR WAR

INDIANA
PURDUE
LIBRARY
FORT WAYNE

JK
1974.7
.B688
1985

Howard S. Brembeck

Imperial Printing Company, 1985

INDIANA
PURDUE
LIBRARY
FORT WAYNE

i

INDIANA-PURDUE
LIBRARY

WITHDRAWN

FORT WAYNE

6

The Alternative to Nuclear War

Copyright © 1985, by Howard S. Brembeck

All rights reserved: This book may not be reproduced in whole or in part, without permission. Inquires should be addressed to the **Alternative World Foundation, Inc.** AWF-1, Goshen, Indiana 46526-0999

Printed by:

Imperial Printing Company
501 Colonial Drive
St. Joseph, MI 49085

PRINTED IN THE UNITED STATES OF AMERICA
First Edition

DEDICATION

To the kind of people who established the United States and those who helped make it what it is: practical dreamers, people who when faced with a problem found a way to solve it.

I am indebted to many such people for helping me develop the Alternative Defense Plan, but one deserves special mention: J. Lawrence Burkholder, president emeritus of Goshen College, a true world citizen, who for over five years kept urging me to keep on with it.

CONTENTS

FOREWORD

The object of this book is to show that there are alternatives to the nuclear arms race and our confrontation with Russia.

The word "Alternative" as used in this book encompasses other ways of looking at things, of thinking, and of acting. Like the mythical Greek sword that cut the Gordian knot, this book strives to cut through the knot of negative thinking and diplomatic complexity surrounding the USA versus USSR confrontation.

The Alternative Defense Plan could solve our present armament dilemma. It spells out how economic power can be used to dethrone military power, reveals how military aggression can be made unprofitable and how nuclear and other mass life-exterminating weapons can be eliminated without any nation losing its sovereignty.

The Alternative Defense Plan is not a detailed blueprint, but a road map for reaching a place on which to build a house to serve as a refuge for all mankind from the offensive weapons of modern war.

An Unprecedented World Problem

Introduction

An Unprecedented World Problem

"To create a problem and not correct it creates an even greater problem."

In 1945, by creating an atomic-powered weapon, the United States brought to the world a problem without precedent. It might have been expected that, having the imagination and energy to create such a devastating weapon, the U.S. would also have the intelligence and discipline to control or remove it. This has not been the case.

Consequently, the United States has to create more nuclear weapons to protect itself against the offspring of the original bomb, which has been produced and multiplied by many other nations.

The problem facing the United States and other nations that have embraced nuclear weaponry is how to give it sanctuary without being consumed by it. It's like living permanently in the same room with a man-eating tiger.

"If you continue to feed a tiger, eventually he will eat you as well." – Chinese proverb

Albert Einstein said, "You can't prepare for war and simultaneously prevent it. Past thinking and methods didn't prevent world war. Future thinking must prevent war." This statement by a very intelligent man causes us to ponder the character of our defense. What can we do to make a nuclear war impossible? Can we destroy nuclear weapons or is it inevitable that we will be destroyed by them?

CHAPTER 1

By Way of Explanation

I

By Way of Explanation

The Alternative Defense Plan has roots that may go back as far as Yalta, Potsdam, Churchill's Iron Curtain speech, the building of the Berlin Wall, or the Berlin blockade. More likely it is the total of these, including a book I read during the early part of World War II entitled *The Coming War and the Rise of Russia* by Dr. Harry Rimmer. It was copyrighted in 1940, but by the time I received my copy, Germany had overrun Western Europe and was bombing England, and Mussolini had invaded Ethiopia. Although he made no mention of the United States or Russia entering the war, the author predicted that Germany would be defeated by Britain and Russia. This interested me, because at that time Germany and Russia had a nonaggression pact to divide up Eastern Europe. Dr. Rimmer predicted Russia's rise to power would come about by her absorbing other nations; those mentioned in particular were all the Balkan nations; and he further went on to say, "Ethiopia and Libya will be independent allies of Russia." The accuracy of these predictions, years ahead of accomplished fact, so intrigued me that I could not help but watch with amazement Russia's rise to power. Little came to my attention about Russia or written by Russians that I didn't read. I sought out people, who had escaped or emigrated from Russia, to discuss life in this totalitarian state. (Several times Dr. Rimmer made reference to Iran or Persia, as it was previously called, becoming part of the Russian empire. It will be interesting to see whether this prediction also proves correct.)

While I was vacationing in England in 1979, riding on a bus, half-asleep, a picture came into my consciousness that I knew afterwards was no ordinary dream. The experience was too vivid, too detailed, too commanding to be a dream and it was similar to an experience that I had had previously, which proved to be a major turning point in my life. It is said that the subconscious is always ahead of the conscious; it was as if my subconscious computer, which had been digesting information for nearly forty years, was making a printout to my conscious mind. It was like watching a play. The two main characters were nuclear physicists: one, definitely Russian, and the other, American. They were talking about destroying all the nuclear bombs they had created.

At dinner that night, I described in detail to the people at my table the "play" that I had seen; it had included two other people besides the two scientists who were both tall, handsome, young looking men.

To the side of them was a shorter, more stockily built Russian and in back of them stood a rather tall, attractive Russian woman, old enough to be the mother of the Russian men. The American scientist, speaking to the Russian scientist but turning to the shorter man, said, "You expect this brother of yours to be the head of your government; can't you persuade him to destroy your bombs?"

The Russian scientist replied, "You don't understand. He can't, I can't, but you can." At this point he appeared to be pleading with the American to help him and his brother, by doing what they could not do.

One person at our dinner table said, "I think you got too much Shakespeare." We had seen one of Shakespeare's plays the night before at Stratford. But I responded, "I haven't thought about Russians or nuclear bombs for a month. Why would my mind design a play around these now?"

"We were at Coventry. Wouldn't that suggest bombs to you?" someone asked.

"Perhaps. But I'm still puzzled," I said, lying a bit

because I felt sure now that I knew the message my subconscious mind had been trying to get my conscious mind to accept.

Two days later I flew across the English Channel to visit our manufacturing plant in Belgium. Looking down on the coast as we approached the continent, my thoughts turned to the Normandy invasion of World War II and the many young American boys who sacrificed their lives for the cause of freedom.

Our Belgium plant distributes our product to all Western European nations; and it occurred to me that, for the first time, all of these countries were democracies. It had been touch-and-go in Portugal, where we had a licensee, but democracy had eventually prevailed. This proved that democracy can win against Communist strategy. Although Western Europe had a Common Market and NATO, it seemed to me that the Western European nations were letting Russia bully them. I felt they didn't realize their own strength and often appeared to consider it more important to please Russia than their sister democracies. If only, I thought, they were more united and more dedicated to democracy, they could tell Russia where to get off.

Our company had been bullied into trying to do business with Russia. We exhibited our products in Moscow. The Russians inspected them, took pictures and made what we felt to be condescending gestures towards doing business, but the red tape and getting all the approvals got to be too much, so we suspended trade relations before we even started them. The suspension of trade with distributors who were constantly creating problems was a practice we had used successfully for many years to resolve malpractices.

Flying back to the United States, I replayed my experience on the bus in England, trying to make sure that I had correctly interpreted the true import of the message trying to be conveyed to my consciousness. Clearly the Russian scientist thought that the American scientist had a better chance of persuading their governments to destroy nuclear bombs than he did.

Knowing the Russian system, how solidly all individuals are cast in this system, even including the President of the Politburo, this made sense. Khrushchev's adventurism and talk of complete disarmament had proven this point. But how would the American scientist do it? In a free society he is permitted to pressure his government, but how would his government in turn pressure the Russian government to agree to the elimination of nuclear weapons? I asked myself these questions: What do the Russians want most from us, the democracies? What do the democracies most want from Russia?

Having studied Russia, I felt sure the thing she most wanted from the democracies was trade, particularly in high-tech products. But I was also convinced she wanted freedom from nuclear weapons. The thing that the democracies most wanted from Russia, I felt, was an effective agreement to eliminate nuclear weapons and armed aggression. Would Russia agree to give up armed aggression for unrestricted access to Western technology, if the agreement included the complete elimination of all nuclear weapons? Extremely unlikely. Why should she, when she can now have both armed aggression and the Western technology? Why should the democracies let her have it both ways, when what they want is the elimination of armed aggression? Western high-tech is a good bargaining point for the democracies. We should offer Russia two things she wants very much – unrestricted access to Western technology and the elimination of nuclear weapons – in exchange for one thing, terminating armed aggression. The democracies would be gaining from the exchange two things – the elimination of nuclear weapons and halting of armed aggression. It would be a good deal all the way around if it could be maneuvered, but it would take some doing, more than we can presently expect from international diplomacy. It would require a sustained cry from the people for liberation from the threat of nuclear weapons and armed aggression. But this pressure would have to be transmitted to Russia in a way that would persuade her to cooperate.

What a beautiful formula! Almost like $E = mc^2$, but bureaucrats would never buy that. It's too simple. If only, I thought, we could get the physicists and the bureaucrats to swap jobs for one year. In that time, the physicists would have ordered all nuclear bombs dismantled and their fissionable materials reprocessed for use in power plants and the bureaucrats wouldn't have made any more bombs because they would still be discussing what kind and how many to make.

Getting back home, I involved myself heavily in my business, trying to forget what I had experienced on the bus; but I found there was no escape, no relief, not even for one day. In 1979 it was hard to get anybody to talk about nuclear bombs. Disarmament was a dirty word and whenever I mentioned suspension of trade as an inducement for Russian disarmament, people immediately thought of it as a boycott, which I found also to be a dirty word because of the connotation that it has acquired, implying the use of force. In the Alternative Defense Plan, no physical force of any kind is involved; instead it's like telling your neighbor with a craving for cookies that, as long as he keeps that man-eating dog in his yard, you're not going to bring him any cookies.

A few people were sympathetic and exhibited interest in my plan. One of them, a college president, was emphatic that I search and research the feasibility of the goal with which I had been presented. Taking his advice, I immediately made this search an important part of my occupation and asked others to help me. I still consider the search an ongoing process, but after five years am pleased to offer for your consideration the thoughts expressed in the following chapters which outline the Alternative Defense Plan.

Thinking it Over

II

Thinking It Over

*"All the problems of the world
could be easily settled, if men were
only willing to think."*
—Nicholas Murray Butler

Before we start to look for any plans or strategies, let us first evaluate our present position and how we got there. The axiom, "If you have a problem, you can be sure that you have done something wrong,'' may apply to the threatening situation in which we find ourselves. So let us reach back a bit in history:

By forsaking our beliefs and commitment to freedom at the end of World War II, transferring territorial rights to a despot heading a government as tyrannical as the one just defeated, the United States told the world it was not committed to its beliefs (excepting as they applied to its own people) and that it was willing to sacrifice the rights of others when it was expedient and served its self-interest. At the end of World War II, we had the power to insist that nations caught in the war between Germany and Russia be given their freedom, but we lacked the courage and the will to use it. The United States, the leading democracy, the proponent of freedom and rule by the ballot, the opponent of rule by the gun, never even asked that a vote be taken to see if the Eastern European nations wanted to be ruled by the Soviet Union. Had we finished the job, seeing to it that all European nations run over by

Germany were given their freedom, we might not have the confrontation with Russia that we have today.

Even then, many, myself among them, were shocked and disillusioned when we learned the deal our government made with Stalin at the end of World War II. I remember someone saying, "How can Roosevelt not know that he is dealing with a devil equally as bad as Hitler? Doesn't he know that Stalin has killed more people than Hitler? Hasn't he read Marx or Lenin? It's unbelievable that he should not know these things; it's public knowledge. He probably didn't read Hitler's *Mein Kampf* either. Hitler told us what he was going to do. We could see with our own eyes what he was doing, yet we would not believe."

It didn't take the Leninist leaders of Russia long to realize that the United States was not fully committed to its beliefs, and they could, with impunity, force their tyrannical rule over other nations. In bowing to tyranny and enslavement we gave the Russian government a false impression of our dedication to freedom, sinned against the founding fathers of the United States who established the democracy which gives us the freedom that we enjoy and sowed the seeds of World War III, which will be the inevitable result if aggression is not brought to a halt.

Believing that the Russians' pattern of thinking is like ours has contributed greatly to our helping the Russians create their empire and their mammoth war machine. Had we really understood them and heeded what Lenin said, the world today might be much less dangerous. It might have been possible for us to have deterred armed occupation of Hungary and Czechoslovakia had Russia known in advance that this would mean complete severance of commercial relations with the United States.

I mention these things to emphasize that the confrontation existing between the Soviet Union and the United States has two parents, not one. We supplied the bomb and opened the door for Russia to create her empire. We still don't understand the Russian mind and we still don't stand as strongly for democracy and freedom as Russia does for communism and slavery. We have continued to consent to Russian aggression and at Helsinki gave it respectability. What we don't consent to, we give through negotiation, without receiving comparable value in return, or as Jean-Francois Revel has said, "We deliberately adopt policies most favorable to the Russians."

Russian propaganda is clever. Not being constrained by Judeo-Christian ethics, she has used them effectively against the democracies to nail them to their own cross. She has conditioned the democracies into giving her what she wants without reciprocity as if it is her due and their responsibility to support Communist aggression.

Armed aggression is central to Russia's foreign policy, not just because it is a characteristic of totalitarianism, but because of Lenin's command to conquer the world. Some think they are on schedule, possibly a little ahead of schedule. Today it's Afghanistan; tomorrow, Iran; the next day, possibly Turkey, who knows? We do know that she has followed a policy of subjugating border nations. China may have to be an exception. Through other nations whose governments she controls, today it is Cuba and Nicaragua; tomorrow, perhaps El Salvador, then Honduras, Costa Rica and Panama. Today in Africa, it's Angola and Ethiopia; tomorrow, it may be other nations which the Soviets can conquer with the help of other Communist nations. There probably is no exact schedule or time table such as this, even in the Kremlin, but the handwriting is on the wall for all the democracies to see if they open their eyes and have the courage to face reality. As with cancer, Communism is a creeping, debilitating disease that moves into areas of the world body that are weak and defenseless, particularly those areas that have been made weak by internal strife or external war. This makes us wonder if Iran may not be the next target for further expansion of the Soviet empire. This crippling political disease likes to move into areas where the surgeon is afraid to use his knife. In other words, the Soviets will move into areas where they feel that the United States or the other democracies will think it is not worth the effort to try to thwart their establishment of Communist rule-by-the-gun governments.

Whether this aggression be territorial annexation through use of military power or installation of governments loyal to Moscow, should not the halting of aggression be central to the strategy of the democracies to prevent fulfillment of Lenin's order for a totalitarian world? Lenin could not have foreseen the nuclear bomb, so it will be up to the democracies to make Russia realize that Lenin's command is not viable in today's world and should they continue to pursue it, the result would be a catastrophic nuclear war.

Returning to our present position, we find ourselves confronting a nation that stands solidly opposed to us politically and economically, with a war machine at least as large as ours, and dedicated to an ideology that avows our destruction. If we consider the wars on the peripheries of influence realistically, the United

States and the Soviet Union, although not proclaimed, are at war now. Throughout history, such confrontations have inevitably led to all-out war.

Victory is likely to favor the totalitarian state with its aggressive, conquer-the-world ideology versus an open democratic society which is not oriented toward war. Democracies are extremely vulnerable to totalitarian state propaganda and war strategy. If war is to be avoided, the open society must devise a strategy for preventing it.

Consider Einstein's "the splitting of the atom has changed everything except man's thinking." Could he have meant that we should think of the nuclear bomb as an instrument of peace rather than of war? Could the awesomeness of the nuclear bomb open man's mind to the realities of war? Let us allow our thinking about the nuclear bomb reach out to strategies that could eliminate not only nuclear weapons but all offensive weapons capable of mass destruction, including chemical and biological weapons. Could this tool have been placed in our hands to prevent another world war? It is a little difficult for us to comprehend this kind of thinking, for the United States did not suffer the ravages of the last two world wars; but, for the Russians who suffered greatly especially in the last war, this could make sense.

The Russians demonstrated how nuclear weapons can be used politically when they took nuclear missiles to Cuba and, before removing them, extracted from the United States a guaranteed sanctuary in the Western Hemisphere. By placing their SS-20 nuclear weapons on their western border, the Soviets doubtlessly hoped to dislodge the United States from Western Europe. This was glaringly revealed by the Russian negotiator Mr. Kvitsinky, just before the Russians walked away from the arms control talks, when he told our Paul Nitze: "You have no business in Europe!"

The Russians have used and still are using the scare value of nuclear weapons with great success in Western Europe, although the danger of their use in Europe is considerably less than in the United States. Russia knows that nuclear war against Western Europe would also mean war with the United States. Why should it want to destroy what would ultimately fall to it as a gift if it directed its fire power against its chief enemy, the United States? Yet through her propaganda and KGB, Russia has made the Western European nations believe they will suffer the effects of nuclear weapons. Admittedly, they are in peril, but the danger is loss of freedom, not devastation from nuclear weapons.

Realizing the awesome power of the nuclear bomb, it is extremely unlikely that either the United States or the Soviet Union will deliberately use it, unless severely provoked. But there it stands - a monument to man's murderous nature - awaiting its call to action.

With the best arms control agreements imaginable, unless supported by an international police force with power and control greater than any one nation or group of nations to enforce total compliance, people will live in the constant fear of this monstrous weapon. Although a less likely target than the United States, Western Europeans are closer to Russia's nuclear weapons. Knowing Russia's intense political and economic propaganda in Western Europe, we can understand why Western Europeans sometimes vent their frustrations on the United States. The resulting misunderstandings have increased Russia's political presence in Western Europe without an equivalent political presence of the Western European nations in the Warsaw pact nations.

Fortunately we have informed, intelligent people in Western Europe, in the United States and people from and inside Russia who warn us that our nation is in peril. Andrei Sakharov, the famous Russian nuclear physicist, told us, "If war is to be prevented, the United States must spend the billions that are necessary to provide the deterrent." Even though the use of nuclear weapons is unthinkable, we need these weapons at the present to offset Russia's threat to us and Western Europe. Will this nuclear armament standoff work for totalitarianism or democracy?

For the first time in this century, all nations of Western Europe have democratic governments. This should be a big advantage in negotiating a meaningful disarmament agreement, if the democracies stand together against totalitarian threats. The bottom line for Russia is to be able to intimidate other nations into doing what she wants. But if the free nations of Western Europe allow themselves to be seduced by Russian propaganda, war between the United States and the Soviet Union would be inevitable. The United States has a commitment to freedom and would fight to the death to preserve it. We must never allow Russia to forget that twice in recent history we have gone to war to preserve freedom in Western Europe and we would again.

Comparing the free enterprise system as practiced by the United States with the Leninist-Stalin totalitarian economic system as practiced by Russia, the free enterprise system appears to be, by far, the most productive of human good. In fact, Russia depends heavily on free enterprise to support its inefficient economic system.

The United States and Russia have some common problems. Maybe these are part of the combination for unlocking the nuclear weapons dilemma. Both spend an enormous amount of money on armament year after year. Instruments of war produce nothing beneficial to mankind; rather they consume precious materials, human life and labor. Building and maintaining arms diminishes mankind's quality of life and is a threat to his existence. In short, building products for war is bad economics. Those who fear converting from war products to products for people would damage the economy should not worry but rather rejoice, for this has never proven to be a problem. Germany and Japan stand as living proof that conversion of this kind can be highly profitable. It could also help the United States be more productive of human needs.

Many different arguments are given for not producing a nuclear weapons defense system. Admittedly, a nuclear weapons defense system would add another dimension to the arms confrontation but, taking the long view, such a system seems inevitable. The argument that it would cause Russia to add a new arms capability doesn't square with the facts. "Since 1972,

Russia has spent as much on 'Star Wars' and other defensive measures as they have on offensive weaponry." – Caspar Weinberger, April 11, 1985.

Another argument is that there can be no perfect defense against nuclear missiles. Every living creature on this earth has developed a defense system or it would not be here. Yet no creature has ever developed the perfect defense system. Nature gives its creatures the intelligence and ability to develop a defense system sufficient to insure their continued existence, but not so perfect as to be invulnerable to certain predators under certain conditions.

A defense system of some kind will be created against nuclear weapons. Self protection is a natural response to threat. Should the United States decide not to develop a nuclear defense capability, all it would be doing is to leave itself vulnerable to nuclear and political threat. Such a decision would not restrain but would rather encourage Russia to accelerate its nuclear defense program and who can say this is wrong? Is it not better than building offensive weapons?

In thinking about nuclear offensive or defensive capability, the thing many people forget is that *Russia is more political than military*. Should she be able to attain a defensive capability over other nations, she would hold a devastating political club over them.

It would be the irony of ironies if the nation that first developed the atomic bomb allowed itself to be destroyed by this weapon because it did not build a defense against it. I believe that both defensive and retaliatory capabilities against nuclear weapons are, for the present at least, equally necessary to maintain a military balance of power. Let him who would complain about the cost put a price on life and liberty.

Let us consider other reasons for the confrontation between the United States and the Soviet Union. Unlike the Western democracies, until recently Russia never had an empire; now, having an empire and the largest war machine on earth is a heady feeling. When you add an ideological, powerful, totalitarian government and helpful enemies, critical of themselves and each other and with no world plan, why shouldn't it be "go" for Russian world control?

The Russian plan for reaching their goal is not understood by most Americans, particularly those who have not read Lenin. Most Americans think in terms of actual warfare - a clash of arms between the United States and Russia. The Russians think quite differently; to them, nuclear weapons are just another tool in their bag of tricks to scare enemies. It is not surprising that, as an aggressor nation, they recognized almost immediately the political value of this weapon, as evidenced by their action in Cuba. Compared to the war policy of the United States which is reactionary, the Russian strategy is long term. Like the chess players they are, their goal is to position themselves through their first move for the more important second or third moves.

Normally they never give up ground gained, but they might give a little to avoid a war with a formidable enemy. It would only be temporary, however, for they will be back another day to move the rock back where they had it, or to advance it further. Lenin warned them against going to war against a powerful opponent, for this could fragment their empire and cause it to crumble. Their plan to subdue the democracies is much more subtle. It's designed to weaken the will of the democracies to resist, through propaganda and KGB activities.

The use of propaganda and ideological warfare is a necessity for totalitarianism to pacify its own people and lure those it has not yet subjugated. As I write, the headline of my daily paper reads, ''Scared Public Looks for Hope at Arms Talks.'' Keeping the Americans and particularly the Western Europeans scared is one of the aims of the Russian propaganda machine. It correctly assumes that the more scared our people are, the more pressure they will apply on the negotiators we send to the arms talks and the better will be their chances of making a deal favorable to themselves. The democracies must realize that, for the Russians, negotiations and treaties are just another form of war.

Coexistence is, I feel, a more realistic goal than peaceful coexistence. The word ''peace'' for totalitarianism has an entirely different meaning than it does for democracy. For the democracies, it means conditions where the integrity of the opposing parties is preserved and neither is trying to subjugate the other. For totalitarianism, peace means conditions where the opposing party has been rendered incapable of resistance.

The Russians are obviously as anxious as we to stay alive. But considering the magnitude of the confrontation and the fact that nuclear weapons are a major part of each nation's armament arsenal, is this possible for any length of time? The war between totalitarianism and democracy exists and will continue. Let us not make the fatal mistake of thinking that this confrontation will dissolve of itself. The only solution is disarmament. If it comes by agreement, it will mean life for all. If by war, it will be death for all.

For the present, coexistence is the first order of importance for both; therefore, let us assume that both equally desire the elimination of nuclear weapons and are willing to make concessions, but the odds of governments achieving this goal of their own volition are about as good as a flower growing on a busy city sidewalk. Governments are too power-oriented, too jealous of their sovereignty, and too frozen in their bureaucratic cast. Government thinking, as a whole, is monolithic and almost moblike. How then can nuclear weapons be eliminated and existence for both democracy and totalitarianism be preserved? Obviously, the thrust for nuclear disarmament will have to come from the people who are in constant danger of losing their lives. They will need to find a way to pressure their governments to work towards nuclear disarmament. But for people in totalitarian states, this will be extremely difficult; so the task will have to be undertaken by people of the democracies. They can influence their governments which, in turn, must influence the totalitarian governments. Success in persuading both types of governments to agree upon a plan to effectively free the world of nuclear and other offensive weapons depends upon the people's ability to initiate and support such an effort. "Private organizations anticipate the future, but government agencies seem to live in the past." — Albert Einstein

Since the Civil War, liberating forces have been at work in the United States and other democracies. When these forces first appear, they are strongly resisted by the majority which fears change. Today, liberation from the terror of devastating weapons of war seems like an idealistic dream, but so it was with every liberation movement: women's suffrage, union rights, laws prohibiting discrimination based on race or sex, etc. The right for people to live free from the fear of death by weapons of war has greater value for mankind than any of the other rights mentioned. No government has the right to take human life without just cause. Government is too important to leave to politicians; there is yet time for the voice of the people to be heard, and that time is *now*. In other words, a Magna Carta of the people forcing their governments to give them their inherent right to live free from the constant threat of nuclear annihilation.

How do we make our voices heard? There is a way. There is an alternative to our present arms course. There is an alternative to nuclear war. There is an alternative to living under the constant threat of nuclear annihilation. There is an Alternative Defense Plan. It is explained in the following chapters.

CHAPTER III

Realities

III

Realities

"Reality — the supreme good."
— Ralph Waldo Emerson

Like Emerson, I believe that reality is the right tool to solve problems. Like a bright light, it exhibits what is real and dispels illusions. This book strives to reveal what is real; this is difficult, for we live in a world where shadows are often mistaken for the real thing.

To many, the Alternative way of thinking is not acceptable; for it often runs counter to accepted thought, prejudice, and practice. But for adventurous, uninhibited, realistic thinkers, it can be provocative and exciting. Here are some realities which may help us get started on our path toward solving the life or death problem to which this book is addressed.

1. For the first time in his history, man has the power to completely destroy his species. It is estimated that he presently has enough nuclear power to kill every man, woman, and child fourteen times.
2. Never in world history has there been a confrontation of the magnitude existing between the United States and Russia. Realistically, a state of war already exists. This can be seen on the perimeters of the spheres of influence. We are caught in a war between two economically and politically incompatible ideologies. Economically, we have Karl Marx warring against Adam Smith. Politically, we have totalitarianism warring against democracy.
3. Technologically our world is now one society, one nation; and the two superpowers in confrontation are warring for control of the world nation. If either attains a definite armament advantage over the other that could be exploited politically or militarily, it could subject the other nation to its rule.
4. Man, like other animals, has an innate character

and social structure which he seems helpless to change. His history has been the tribe, the feudal or city-state, the nation, and presently it's the nation-group. All of these were formed for reasons of security, for dominance or the establishment of law. These primordial forces are at work today setting the stage for establishing law in a lawless world. It is unrealistic to believe that these forces will stop short of an attempt at world control. What we decide now will determine the character of world control. Many think that this is some time in the distant future. Others believe this decision could be reached before the year 2000.

5. Humans, like many other animals, are very territorial minded. Aggression or the use of military power by one nation against another creates a state of war. Severely penalizing aggression, if a good way can be found to do so, should help to keep small wars from developing into a large war.

6. Russians think and act differently than we do; their government follows the teachings of Karl Marx

whose gospel can be summed up in the word "hate": hate anyone who has more than you. Our government follows the Judeo-Christian principle that can be summed up in the word "love": love every person for the good that is in him. Considering these great ideological differences, it isn't surprising that our governments see things quite differently. But the Russian government represents a minority of the Russian people, so we must not allow ourselves to believe that all Russians are as bad as their government would like them to be. They are just as human as we are and, if we don't learn to live with them and show some love for them as people, we will die with them.

7. An alternative to war will have to be one that provides Russia or any other potential aggressor with benefits greater than can be obtained through war.

8. Regardless of what the Russians say, we can count on them (and most other nations) to do what they think is to their advantage. Agreements in a law-

less world are no substitute for military defense. Arms control talks generally have had the effect of producing more and smarter weapons rather than less. Realistically, where control is impotent, arms control talks are just another form of war.

9. Man's real power and glory is economic, not military, power. The United States is a much greater economic power in manmade goods internationally than the Soviet Union. If we used our economic power wisely, in concert with other free industrialized nations, our influence to affect nuclear disarmament would be far greater than it is now. This assumes that we have an adequate deterrent to prevent Russia from launching a war against the democracies.

10. Unilaterally, the United States cannot eliminate nuclear weapons. But, unilaterally, through prudent use of its economic power, the United States can create an international climate in which elimination of nuclear weapons will be likely to take place.

11. Nuclear power, like other great discoveries, can be man's slave rather than his master, if controlled.
12. *IF* controlled: can it be controlled residing in bombs that can be delivered in minutes to a spot thousands of miles away by the press of a button? That is the question facing all mankind.
13. The only realistic refuge from the threat of nuclear war is international law effectively supported by enforcement which prohibits possession by individual nations of nuclear and other mass life-exterminating weapons.
14. *The price for international peace is enforceable international law.*

CHAPTER IV

The Alternative Defense Plan (ADP)

"There is a way — find it."

— Thomas Edison

IV

The Alternative Defense Plan

Preface
"The world of Karl Marx"

The economic woes of the Free World fade when compared with the slow growth and severe pressures facing the 25 Marxist nations, according to the Conference Board, the New

York-based business research group. Marxist countries, it says, from the Soviet Union, China, and Libya to Cuba, account for 40% of the world's population, but only about 10% of its trade. And while many Marxist nations reported growth in 1984, it was often not real. "In many cases economic improvements were mainly the result of accidental short-term factors and a stronger than usual distortion of statistics," notes the author, Josef Adamek. "The centrally planned economies will continue to need Western imports, especially food-stuffs and technology." Countries such as Hungary, Bulgaria, China, East Germany, and Yugoslavia, which have adopted economic reforms or gotten substantial outside aid, will fare better, he says. But the future for most of these economies is bleak, owing to basic inefficiencies, excessive military spending, suppression of human rights (including use of forced labor) and the impact of past policies. The Russians, for example, have 26 million workers, out of 140 million, producing goods for the military and 8.5 million more making military hardware, Adamek says. And his report concludes that the outlook is worse for war-racked nations such as Vietnam, Laos, Cambodia, Afghanistan, Ethiopia, Angola, Mozambique and Nicaragua.

Forbes magazine, January 14, 1985

Others have made similar reports about the Russian economy, but few of the democracies have realized the significance of these evaluations. Russian propaganda has been scaring and bullying them with a weapon she can't use and trying to blind them to the fact that they, not Russia, possess the most powerful weapon — economic power. The beauty of the democracies' weapon is that it is one they can use and it will produce good results, rather than bad. Commerce is man's universal positive power, the creator of his civilizations, his common life support. It is, unfortunately, also the creator and supporter of military power. It's the power wherein the democracies exceed the Soviet Union by a tremendous margin, a margin far greater than their margin in military power. As this is a fact, why don't the democracies employ this weapon to counter totalitarian weapons and propaganda? Doing so would put them on a more equal basis with our bully friend. Friend? We call somebody who threatens to blow us to smithereens a friend? Yes, why not? A person who has an idea to sell doesn't approach his prospect by addressing him as ''my dear enemy''; rather he says, ''My dear friend, I have something that will make you rich.'' His friend says, ''You mean, make you rich.'' You say, ''Well, maybe so, but not so rich as you. We'll both be rich. What's so wrong with that?''

The difference between making a deal and negotiating is in character. In negotiating, parties try to obtain from each other as much as possible and give as little as possible. The problem with negotiation is that it's self-interest rather than mutual-interest oriented. In dealing, all parties join together in a venture to become richer. The best deals are mutually rewarding and self-enforcing. But with any agreement, even though mutually rewarding, men will never live peaceably, without law, until they are under God.

Presently, to reduce the tension and the threat of nuclear war between us and the Soviets, we talk about arms control or a freeze, which are only token measures, when full measures are required if freedom from the threat of nuclear war is our goal. These aspirin type remedies are no cure for problems requiring a full fix. Eliminating nuclear weapons completely would be much easier than trying to control them. There are a number of reasons for this. Complete elimination is impartial and removes all doubt about quantity or kind. An arms control agreement, no matter how well intentioned, written or verified, will forever be a maze of complexity, of judgemental decisions, and a breeding ground for more suspicion, distrust and accusation. If a nation cuts its arsenal of nuclear weapons from 10,000 to 1,000 or 100 or even 10, we must ask ourselves, "Has anything been gained? Why the 10?" We can answer this by reflecting on what we did with

2 atomic bombs in Japan, taking into consideration that thermonuclear bombs today are a thousand times more powerful. If the ultimate objective is to eliminate the 10, why go through years of agonizing, exposing ourselves to the constant risk involved? Does not logic dictate going from 10,000 to 0?

Providing talk is weighted toward solutions for improving the state of man, rather than armament, conferences between nations, both adversaries and allies, should produce mutual benefit. The best agreements may not be those on paper but rather word of mouth, for these words have life and flexibility. Each time they are spoken, they increase in stature and meaning.

Realistically, we know that in a lawless world arms control talks are mostly political staging to pacify the populace, to make them think that something is being done which is not being done and will never be done until our confrontation with the Russians takes on an entirely different character. A change in character of the relationship can only come about by changing the rules of the game. This will have to be initiated by the

United States, if it is to be. What kind of a game am I talking about?

It's a game where everybody wins. Some call it cooperation; some, reciprocity. In simple terms, it's giving others things they want and you have, in exchange for things they have that you want. The result is that both parties are enriched.

Let's make a hypothetical assumption at this point, that the people of the United States have pressured their government for the right to exist free from the fear of nuclear and other life-threatening weapons. And as a result, they have caused it to make a nonviolent unilateral move (quite the opposite of building more offensive weapons) that would pressure the Russians into talking meaningfully about nuclear disarmament. The question now is: Do the United States and other democracies have the courage and the will to use their most effective weapon, and with sufficient pressure, to get Russia and other aggressor nations to cooperate?

If the Alternative Defense Plan is going to effectively control nuclear and other offensive weapons, it will have to be realistic and feasible: It should not try to remake man, but rather evaluate his natural behavior and assume, in the absence of effective law enforcement, he is going to do what he wants to do regardless of what he agrees to do. It should, therefore, be our objective to design a plan that offers the things that he wants at a price he can afford and will be willing to pay.

In creating the Alternative Defense Plan, we must keep in mind that aggression is a disease that feeds on itself and will persist until it is stopped. It's a disease that affects primarily totalitarian governments; fortunately, there are prescriptions that can effectively stop and control potentially deadly diseases. If caught early, aggression, like other diseases, can be brought under control relatively easily. But should it get out of control, stopping it becomes an all-out effort which can be extremely costly. If, for example, Hitler had been stopped when he marched into the Sudentenland or

Austria, World War II might have been avoided. To have stopped him at this point would have required a great effort by the other European nations and the United States but would have been a lot less costly at this point than it was later; so our plan must discourage and make extremely difficult aggression in its early stages.

For the Alternative Defense Plan to succeed in halting aggression, it will need to be one that the Russians can and want to accept, at least eventually. It will need to be a stick-and-carrot approach that applies enough pressure to get the Russians to talk meaningfully about disarmament and holds out enough goodies to whet their appetite. It should also scare them by giving a picture of their future relative position should they choose not to cooperate with the unified democratic nations rather than joining them in a crusade for peaceful coexistence.

To make it appealing to aggressor nations, the plan should be offered in the manner of an invitation to join a save-the-world club and, accurately, list all the benefits offered by joining. Nations have enormous egos. Saving face is extremely important. To have a realistic chance of becoming successful, the plan must factor in these elements. Russia would probably prefer to starve than appear submissive to the democracies. To avoid such a possibility, the plan will need to be so designed and presented that when Russia does join the Alternative aligned nations, she is given a hero's welcome. Due to her historical feeling of inferiority, Russia is sensitive to both flattery and anything that would deflate her ego. In making this declaration or announcement of the Alternative Defense Plan, the United States should take particular care in presenting it to Russia to let her know that it is no design against her (for she will at first almost certainly interpret it as such), but rather a desire to coexist in an environment free from the constant threat of war. It should also stress that, should she join the Alternative aligned nations, all members would be willing to share technology with her and do business on any products she may wish. With effective international enforcement to control offensive weapons, what could the United States and other democracies lose? The biggest loss for the United States would be in jobs for the CIA. Russia would have the same problem in the KGB, for why spy when you can get it for the asking? With offensive weapons under international control, the need for defensive weapons would be very limited. Rather than losing, both gain through trade benefits for their people.

The plan must be nonpolitical, penalizing only aggressor nations that use force to invade the land, sea or air space of another nation and nations that trade with such aggressor nations.

The plan should depend entirely upon nonviolent and voluntary action; no threats or use of arms of any kind.

Except for the proviso that it takes two-thirds of the nations doing two-thirds of the world's international commerce for the Alternative Defense concept to become world law, all nations should be treated equally. No veto power or special privileges for certain nations.

Favoritism by the Alternative Agency could be disastrous. The objective is one law that equally protects all nations.

Why so much talk about aggression and offensive weapons? Are these the hinges on which the Alternative Defense Plan swings? Yes, these are the twin devils that create war. Since the United States was the first nation to make and use nuclear bombs, it should be the first to take a positive step to eliminate them. Therefore, I propose that the United States make the following Declaration:

DECLARATION

To eliminate nuclear and all other civilian life-threatening offensive weapons of war, we support the suspension of trade on man-made goods with nations that use, threaten to use, or supply such weapons and with all nations that trade directly or indirectly with these nations.

If the United States made this proclamation, it would be telling all the world that we believe people have the inherent right to live free from the fear of weapons of war. As did the founders of our nation, I believe that people have inherent rights that employers, governments, or any organization do not have the right to abridge. People are protected by law in the United States and in many other nations from having to work in an environment that endangers their health or lives. Yet at the same time, there are many in these nations contributing their labor, skill, and ingenuity to make things solely to kill people.

Just before World War II, I recall protests against commercial interests selling scrap to Japan, but these were of no avail against the voices proclaiming our need for international trade. As predicted, many American soldiers were killed with steel made in America. Today these same voices are saying, "We must continue trade with Russia regardless of her aggression against other nations."

As an international businessman, it is hard for me

to comprehend the thinking of any businessman who would put trade with aggressor and aggressor-related nations ahead of his own and his family's survival and the survival of his nation. Whatever our line of work, as citizens of the United States, the question is whether or not we are willing to forfeit a relatively small amount of international trade of manufactured goods for the most precious things in the world – life and freedom – for ourselves and those who come after us.

In a democratic society we expect differing opinions, but it is hard to understand the logic of people who think it is all right for Russia to threaten Western Europe with her nuclear weapons but wrong for Western Europe to provide a deterrent to this threat. What is even more difficult to comprehend is the ''logic'' of people who think it is all right for Russia to maintain a military establishment in Cuba and export aggression to Central America and Africa, but improper for us to help these victim nations defend themselves against this military aggression.

If those in power can be convinced that the majority

of the people anxiously desire removal of the cloud of death that hangs over us, this possibility can become reality. Should the United States make such a Declaration as this book proposes, the affect on other free nations of the world could be electric. In one simple stroke, the United States would change its policy of supporting freedom from use of armed force to non-violent enforcement. This would be more effective, certainly less costly, and would involve less risk of provoking war. Suppose, for example, that the Declaration had existed at the time of the Falkland Islands war. It is unlikely that Britain would have needed to send any warships, airplanes or troops to these islands. The price that Argentina would have had to pay for aggression, the loss of all trade in manmade goods with the United States and other democracies, would have been too great compared to the gain.

If the Alternative Defense Plan were in effect now, Nicaragua would probably present no problem for the United States, for it is unlikely that Nicaragua would want to shut itself off completely from all the free industrialized nations and become a captive Soviet satellite like Cuba. There might even be a question in Russia's mind whether she would want to support another Cuba.

The way the Declaration is constructed, the United States can play its role in containing aggression but, by wielding its power in a nonviolent way, can exert it in areas where the use of force of arms would be unwise. Its commitment not to trade in manufactured goods with an aggressor nation or any nation dealing directly or indirectly with an aggressor nation will doubtless cause the U.S. to lose some international trade. It is unlikely, however, that any of the large free industrialized nations will choose the Soviet Union over the United States for their trading partner on manufactured goods; if some do, so be it. The cost of policing aggression with trade will still be much less than with military force. Keep in mind that the plan does not call for restriction of trade in earth products, even with aggressor nations. In event of an actual war of an aggressor nation against any of the Alternative aligned nations, suspension of trade by the Alternative aligned nations with the aggressor nation would also include earth products, making the suspension of trade between all of the Alternative aligned nations against the aggressor nation a complete trade embargo. This feature of the ADP should discourage an aggressor nation from attacking an Alternative aligned nation. It is also a good reason for being a member of the Alternative Alliance.

The Alternative Defense Plan permits the use of naval forces to keep the sea lanes of the world open to trade and the supplying of defensive weapons and advisory personnel to nations under attack by an aggressor nation. Another feature of the ADP is that it allocates the international policing of aggression among all of the Alternative aligned nations, rather than burden one nation with this task.

Why does the Declaration include suspension of trade with nations that are not themselves aggressors but who only trade with aggressor nations? The Declaration would be meaningless if second or third parties were not included in the suspension of trade, for an aggressor nation could always use another nation as an agent through which to purchase their manufactured goods. Trade sanctions that do not go all the way, as we have experienced, probably create more aggravation and animosity than benefit.

Why does the Declaration limit itself to manufactured goods? Why aren't earth products such as oil, minerals, lumber, grains, and foods of all kinds included in the trade restraint order? ADP recognizes manmade or manufactured goods as the guilty party creating the armament problem. It sees no value in restricting trade on earth products; for it sees in them no threat to mankind, but rather a benefit that should not be denied to any people whether they live in an aggressor nation or not. Suspending trade with aggressor nations (as long as they do not resort to nuclear or other mass life-exterminating weapons) on earth products would work against the ultimate objective of the Alternative Defense Plan, which is to make all people richer, healthier, happier, not poorer.

What is the administrative design for the Alternative Defense Plan? For implementation of the Declaration, it is recommended that the United States, assuming that it made the proposed Declaration, establish an Alternative Agency, independent of but located near the United Nations. It would then be convenient for representatives of all nations to visit the Agency and learn about the Alternative Defense Plan. The Alternative Agency is not seen as a competitor but as an independent associate of the United Nations with its activities confined to the control of aggression and offensive weaponry. Weapons judged by the Alternative Agency to be defensive would be exempt.

It is proposed that the terms of the Alternative Defense Plan should contain these provisions: A nation declaring in favor of the Alternative Defense Plan should discontinue the manufacture and supply of all offensive weaponry and withdraw all combat troops on foreign soil within one year from the date of making its Declaration. Not until this has been done should any nation be allowed to invoke the suspension of all trade on manufactured goods with aggressor and aggressor-supplying nations.

A year for preparedness between the date of Declaration and effective date of trade suspension is proposed to allow nations to withdraw combat troops from foreign soil and complete trade contracts. Probably a review board would be needed to consider extension of time on large contracts begun before the effective date of the Declaration that could not be completed within one year. It is assumed, of course, that no increase in the contract would be permitted during this period. This board, with the approval of the governing board, might also consider extreme hardship cases, such as repair parts, medicinals, etc.

The Alternative Defense Plan will use only voluntary and nonviolent means to achieve its goals. All nations can choose whether or not to join with the United States in its Declaration against aggression and for freedom from mass life-exterminating weaponry. A nation making this Declaration, in addition to its own surveillance over trade with aggressor and aggressor-related nations, would be required to help maintain a trade-monitoring investigative body. Its purpose would be to report to the Agency violations of the trade suspension agreement. Should a nation that had joined the Alternative Alliance of Nations be found in violation of the terms of the Alternative, it would be subject to economic sanctions, the severity of which would depend upon the seriousness of the violation. The sanctions would be sufficiently severe that no nation would knowingly violate the terms of the Alternative. A renegade nation that was guilty of serious and frequent violations of the terms of the Alternative would be disfranchised as an Alternative aligned nation and would be obliged to trade solely with aggressor and aggressor-related nations.

While the provisions of the Alternative call for the discontinuance of manufacture and supply of offensive weaponry one year from date of Declaration, there is no prohibition for the Alternative aligned nations against the possession and use *for defensive purposes* of offensive weapons that a nation has on hand at the time its Declaration becomes fully effective, which is one year after announcement. Neither is there any prohibition against the continual development, manufacture and sale of defensive weaponry or the use of advisors to help nations that are threatened militarily during the period of suspension of trade on manufactured goods.

It is expected that when, and if, two-thirds or more of the nations of the world (which would embody the nations doing two-thirds or more of the world's international commerce, including Russia), have joined the non-aggression aligned nations, *the Alternative Defense Plan would become world law*. It would have the authority over possession and use of offensive weapons and the responsibility for methodically destroying all offensive weapons on a pro rata basis. Nations would keep only those weapons determined by the Alternative Agency as necessary to maintain internal order and protect national boundaries. Since the kind of weapons permitted nations or individuals would be controlled by international law, it is conceivable that eventually nothing more lethal than a rifle might be the only legal weapon in the world.

Assuming that two-thirds of the nations of the world doing two-thirds of the world's international commerce joined the Alternative Agency and declared its precepts to be international law, it would follow that an Alternative Enforcement Agency would be required to enforce the law. It would be important that the Alternative Enforcement Agency be a highly competent, professional, international police force recruited from as many as possibly a hundred nations, equipped with the best scientific instruments and military hardware the world has to offer for detecting and suppressing violations of the terms of the Alternative. It would also have the most sophisticated space surveillance available and military power greater than any single nation or group of nations. It would need to have sufficient nuclear weapons to discourage any nation or group of nations from trying to secretly create nuclear bombs or to launch a nuclear attack. Any nation committing such acts could expect to suffer the devastation of a nuclear bomb response. The Alternative Enforcement Agency would keep its nuclear and other arms arsenal under close surveillance and control at all times.

To reduce the risk of any of the Alternative Enforcement Agency personnel being bribed or granted national favors, the term of employment would be limited and there would be a plan for rotation from location to location and from nation to nation. Within the Enforcement Agency, there would be a group of plainclothes personnel, expertly trained for detecting terrorists. Penalties for illegal acts would be severe, both against the terrorists and the nation harboring or sponsoring them. Complete economic isolation is a potent penalty.

Should any nation fear that forfeiting its sovereignty over offensive weaponry would lead to forfeiting its sovereignty in governing itself, it would be stressed that the Alternative Agency's responsibility is restricted exclusively to preventing increase and use of offensive weaponry and to preventing aggression. Nations joining the Alternative Alliance would be exchanging their sovereignty over life-threatening offensive weapons for international protection from such weapons while retaining sovereignty in all other areas. Today the United States, Russia and dozens of other nations are paying a high price for protection from offensive weapons, but, for all they spend, they are not protected. They are still vulnerable and will continue to be until they are willing to turn over to a responsible body the awesome weapons they fear may be used against them.

"A world authority and an eventual world state are not just desirable in the name of brotherhood, they are *necessary* for survival." — Albert Einstein

In the early days in the western part of the United States when there was no law, it was common practice, if not a necessity, for people to carry firearms. After law was established, people were freed of this burden and the ever-present threat of death. It is unlikely that the governments of the United States and Russia will act with similar intelligence without a lot of people pressure. They hang onto their bombs as if their lives depended on them when, in fact, their lives depend upon getting rid of them. How then can they be persuaded to make such an exchange? This is the subject of the next chapter.

Strategy For World Peace

V

Strategy for World Peace

"A break in the established order is never the work of chance. It is the outcome of man's resolve to turn life to account."
— *Andre Malraus*

The grand design of the Alternative Defense Plan is to give birth to an Alternative World in which the democracies and the totalitarian states can coexist without the fear that they are going to be terminated by the other. In short, MAS (Mutual Assured Survival) instead of MAD (Mutual Assured Destruction). It recognizes the differences between these two forms of government and that the ideologies supporting them are already at war with each other. It also recognizes that in any highly contested game, if it were not for rules of play supported by the authority to penalize malpractice, the contestants would probably end up killing each other. This design allows each party to retain its ideology for its own people, and even have the privilege of promoting it with other people, as long as it is done without violating the rules of the game.

The design for getting the rules of the game changed is what we call "The Exchange." It's persuading the government of the United States and the government of Russia to make a deal wherein both would obtain two things of high value in exchange for only one thing of questionable value. Both would receive a guarantee that the lives of their people will not be threatened nor their land devastated. In exchange for forfeiting the right to use armed force against other nations, Russia would receive free access to Western technology and assistance in applying this technology. For this, the democracies would be relieved of the burden of using arms to halt armed aggression. They would, however, still retain the right to help free nations defend themselves against guerrilla or terrorist groups using small arms supplied by aggressor nations. We will probably always have border and civil wars. But, because under the Alternative Defense Plan supplying offensive weapons violates international law, it is unlikely that these wars will develop into a sizeable conflagration. The Alternative Enforcement Agency should be a good fire extinguisher.

Proposed strategy for getting the rules of the game changed is divided into five steps. They are as follows:

1. Inform the people of the United States of the

Alternative Defense Plan and gain support from a sufficient number so that their voice is heard in Congress, the Senate and in the White House.

2. Persuade the United States government to make a Declaration as proposed.
3. Establish the Alternative World Agency and hire high grade personnel for administering and monitoring the terms of the Alternative Defense Plan.
4. Enact the terms of the Alternative into international law when two-thirds of the nations of the world, including Russia, doing two-thirds of the international trade of the world have joined the Alternative World Agency.
5. Create the Alternative Enforcement Agency which would take charge of all nuclear and other weapons determined by the Agency as offensive as soon as the Alternative Defense Plan becomes world law. It would have the responsibility of eliminating all offensive weapons on a scheduled pro rata basis. Parallel to its demolition activities, the Alternative Enforcement Agency should

create its military capability for asserting its authority, which would continue as long as the international law as defined by the Alternative World Agency existed.

As the United States was the first to develop and use an atomic bomb, the Alternative Defense Plan places a lot of responsibility on it in assuming leadership for eliminating nuclear weapons. While aggression may be the element most responsible for the arms race, the United States, nevertheless, because of the nuclear threat involved, should take the first meaningful steps toward resolving this problem, even though it involves applying pressure on the government of the Soviet Union. Certainly, people of the Soviet Union, if they could, would pressure their government as much as the people of the democracies to eliminate nuclear weapons.

The strategy behind the suspension of trade to aggressor and aggressor-related nations is a design to unite the democracies and other free industrialized nations in a creative way, in a way that we feel will make the democracies more self confident and less fearful of the Russian threat. Realistically, trying to get the governments of the free industrialized nations to unite through negotiation, on a trade suspension plan on manufactured goods against aggressor nations would be a practical impossibility. Not that people in government are worse than others but, on the whole, they are so concerned about protecting what they perceive to be their self interests, they could talk forever without reaching a disarmament agreement that would give people real protection. But, by making its Declaration, the United States in one bold stroke makes doing business with it conditional on not engaging in aggression or not doing business directly or indirectly with an aggressor nation.

The terms of the Alternative require that all nations making the Declaration and joining the Alternative Alliance cease to manufacture and supply offensive weapons and withdraw all combat troops from foreign soil within one year from the date of making their Declaration. This courageous strategic move is designed to let the rest of the world know the Alternative Defense Plan's position on offensive weapons. It also lets them know that a nation joining the Alternative Alliance is not put at the mercy of an aggressor nation. There is no prohibition on manufacturing or possessing defensive weapons nor on keeping offensive weapons on hand at the time of making the Declaration.

The strategy against aggression is to sever its roots rather than fight its branches, in the belief that the branches will wither of themselves if the roots are severed. Aggression is an essential element of Leninist Communism. Lenin admitted that economically Communism was not working, that the socialist totalitarian state he envisioned could not solve the internal problems it had created and that it would have to expand or die. Therefore, he made aggression, or living off the fruits of other nations, a tenet of Communist policy. As we have said, Lenin is dead and the nuclear world in which we live today was far beyond his imagination, so it falls upon the democracies to help Russia see that her goals cannot be obtained through aggression, and, that should she continue to pursue this path, a major war is inevitable. It also falls upon the democracies to help Russia economically, but this must not be a one-sided deal as in the past. For technological and other economic help, the democracies should demand reciprocal accommodation in the form of freedom from the threat of weapons of war.

The difference between Communism and democracy is that democracy is based in law while Communism is based on the reach for unbridled power by a few over many. The democracies can't do much about Russia's form of government over its own people, but they can stand solidly together on a suspension of trade until Russia agrees not to use force of arms in her reach for world power. Many Americans think that she will never abandon armed aggression, but study of her behavior indicates that she is quite realistic as well as pragmatic. What she can gain through military aggression and her mammoth war machine, large as it is, does not compare in value to the guarantee of freedom from the threat of nuclear weapons and the opportunity to gorge herself on the technological goodies of the Western candy store of technology.

How will the free industrialized nations react to the Declaration of the United States? Some will probably applaud us for taking a courageous stand; others may try gentle persuasion to get us to reverse our stand. Many, maybe the majority, will denounce us even while admitting that a nation, like a person, has the right to trade what they wish, with whom they wish, for whatever reasons they feel are important to them. Withholding trade or services is the most common form of action in the world to get other people to cooperate with you, to get them to give you what you want. Unions use it every day to get employers to grant them things they feel are important, and every person almost daily uses it in purchasing goods or services. Although it usually requires both parties to give up something they would rather keep, it's a beneficial form of action because it gives both parties things that they want more than the things they surrender. Certainly this would be true for both the United States and Russia.

After making our Declaration, I expect that the following scenario will result. The great majority of the free industrialized nations will eventually join the United States in the Alternative Alliance of Nations. At first, there will be holdouts, but through persuasion and the pressure of economics, these nations will eventually join the crusade to abolish nuclear weapons. Since there is no prohibition on trade of earth products and Russia has little to offer in manufactured goods, it is expected that few nations will choose Russia for their trading partner, and those few will not be large in international trade.

The United States will need to use diplomacy in dealing with the free nations that complain that the suspension of trade on manufactured goods is hurting them. We should, where possible, help them to find other markets or sources of supply within the community of free industrialized nations. It should also level with them and ask them which they think is more important — the loss of some trade on manufactured goods or their lives. The nuclear confrontation between the United States and the Soviet Union cannot be over exaggerated. It is real. It is the greatest threat to survival that mankind has ever faced. The chief administrator for the Alternative World Agency should have on his desk a motto like one that I saw on the desk of a president for a company fighting for survival. It read, ''If you think we can continue to do business as usual while others here are pulling their hair, possibly you don't realize the situation.''

When the Alternative Alliance becomes reality and a majority of the nations have joined it and others are on the brink of joining, Russia will likely become very vocal and try to convince other holdout nations that she is being cornered and coerced by the United States. She probably will threaten war, spout a lot of venomous talk and make calculated warlike gestures, but will stop short of actual war.

Some fear that Russia might react to a trade sanction

by declaring war even though she is offered the same opportunity as every other nation. This is highly improbable, for it is contrary to Russia's past behavior and Leninist policy. Unlike our policy which is reactionary, Russia's is a long-term design. Moreover, she is too vulnerable and has too much to lose in a war against formidable enemies. Lenin told them that capitalist nations, because of their greed for money, will carry on commerce at any cost. Realizing the fragility of national alliances and the ineffectiveness of most previous trade sanctions, Russia will never believe that the Alternative Alliance will hold together. And she has been too successful in circumventing trade sanctions in the past to feel seriously threatened. She is more apt to lick her chops as she thinks about the United States terminating the manufacture of offensive weapons.

Was Lenin right? Are the democracies so dedicated to doing business as usual that they will not pay the price (forego some profit on a limited amount of international trade) to preserve their lives and their freedom? Or are they so blind, so greedy, that they will sell their souls and give the bodies of their children to slavery or to be burned for a few dollars? Have they lived in freedom so long that they have forgotten that it always comes at a price, often an extremely high price as in World War II. Today freedom from nuclear weapons can be purchased at a reasonable price, a price that we can afford. Tomorrow freedom from nuclear weapons may not be available at any price.

Let us hope and pray that the great majority of the free industrialized nations stand solidly together, forfeiting some profit if that is necessary, to obtain the greatest profit our world has to offer — life without the constant fear of annihilation. If they do, and this will depend mostly on the determination of the United States to see that nuclear weapons are eliminated, the flow of manufactured goods and technology from the free nations to the aggressor and aggressor-related nations will probably be reduced to a trickle. Then Russia, starting with a per capita income well below the average of the free industrialized nations, will get increasingly further behind economically the longer she holds out. Likewise, the nations under Russia's control will eventually feel the pinch if they are not able to trade with the free industrialized nations. This could put the brakes on establishing further beachheads through aggression.

What about the Eastern European nations that are quite highly industrialized and Russia herself? Won't they be able to carry on and support themselves and the other nations under Russian domination on a comparable basis to the West? They probably could if they had a free competitive economic system; but, under the Russian totalitarian economic system and without the support of the free industrialized nations, it would be next to impossible. The reason for this is in one word: competition. Without it, no economic system can be highly productive. Even with all the financial help and technology that the Western nations have given to Russia and her satellites, except for producing a mammoth war machine, she has accomplished nothing worthy of note in the field of manufacturing. The democracies should not worry about Russian competition in technology, for she has not shown any expertise at putting it to wide use. Rather they should look to her as a future customer for their technology and as a good source of supply for earth products.

Those who have studied or negotiated with Russia have no illusions about the difficulty of selling her on the Alternative Defense Plan. Change in Russia comes hard and slow. Economic benefit takes second place to ideology. But time has a way of changing things that are thought to be unchangeable. Economically, Russia is on a dead end street. In ten to fifteen years, without the support of the free industrialized nations, the difference in the standard of living in Russia and her trading partners in contrast to that in the Alternative aligned nations will be so evident that Russia will consider joining the Alternative Alliance. And, if the Alternative aligned nations employed a "friendship offensive," she might join much earlier. This offensive would be basically an attitude that would prompt the nations of the Alternative Alliance to tell Russia that we sincerely want them with us, and to review the advantages. The Alternative aligned nations should find the friendship offensive a good investment. Although secluding themselves behind walled borders, Russians, by nature, are gregarious people. They like to belong and want to be a part of the world community.

The next twenty years could see an economic entrepreneurship explosion in India and China comparable to what we have seen in Japan, Korea, Taiwan and some of the other Far Eastern nations. If this materializes, Russia's influence over other great powers of the world will diminish. This is because she has built her empire upon Lenin's philosophy that power flows from the barrel of a gun. Although neither we nor the Russians yet realize it, this axiom may already be obsolete. Man's real power, as we observe, is economic, not military. Modern technology will obsolete many weapons. Russia has had a taste of world power. It is unlikely that this thirst will slacken or she will want to watch her world influence erode while China's, India's, and the other democracies' increase. Since war is no longer a viable pathway to influence and power, Russia's best hope for maintaining her status is to join the Alternative nations, for they can give her the technological assistance to help her hold her position with China, her Communist competitor.

No one knows, of course, what Russia's reaction would be to our Declaration. Being our adversary, she probably will think it a move against her. And should she think that way, we will have to try to convince her that our unilateral action is directed toward freeing the world from the threat of nuclear weapons and aggression that we feel might lead to a devastating war between our two great nations.

We all are aware of the desire in many of the democracies to go for a quick solution, such as a freeze. But any solution that gives only temporary relief may well be worse than none at all. It could lead people into believing that the problem had been solved when all we had done was to stick our heads in the sand. To solve a large problem, we must stand back from it far enough so that we can see it as a whole, not just count the kinds and number of trees in the forest. The confrontation between the USA and the USSR has been long in building. It has assumed tremendous proportions. It is going to take time, patience, understanding, and a determined effort to restructure it for continued coexistence.

Appeasement leads to war, for eventually it puts the appeaser in a corner where he has to fight or capitulate. Few of us can imagine the United States going down without a fight, even if it means a fight to the death.

For nations, people and many forms of animal life, boundaries are necessary for peaceful coexistence. When aggression occurs, fighting follows. Internally, nations establish laws that penalize people who violate the rights of others. But, externally, nations can indulge in aggression, disregarding the rights of other nations, without penalty. Penalizing aggression is basic in the animal kingdom, of which we are a part, to secure peaceful coexistence.

With the ending of aggression, it has been proven that formerly aggressive nations turn from machines of destruction to producing things that help people live at a higher level. Japan is a good example. Defeated in an all out effort to conquer with military might, she turned to making products for consumers. It was here that she found her true power and glory, and through it has conquered the world in a way unimaginable with military power. "Conquering" the world through commerce has brought prosperity to the Japanese people and international respect to her as a nation. Today, her yen is one of the most valued currencies. At the same time, she has provided people throughout the world with valuable products that they need. And she has done all this without sacrifice to her people.

If any doubt exists that war is not the way, let us, by contrast, consider Russia. Victorious in war, she has continued to pursue her goal through war. Today she sits on a mountain of military junk. Her people live in want and slavery. Scarcity, deceit and suspicion stalk her land and every nation on which she has laid her imperialistic hand. She manufactures few goods acceptable to the world market. Her ruble has little international value. Feared by other nations, she continues to infect the weak ones with her paranoid war ways through the use of the gun. What an opportunity for the United States to use its economic power, combined with that of other free industrialized nations, to make Russia realize that war does not pay.

It's possible that Russia will not turn from her aggressive ways until she has a freer society. People kept in confinement behind walls, not permitted to travel outside their nation, people denied ownership of property, people denied the opportunity to express their creativity and energy other than through government prescribed rules of order, become frustrated. Frustration can express itself in many ways, belligerency, aggressiveness, unwillingness to cooperate, etc. This could be a Russian characteristic for some time. During this period we will need to man our ramparts, but we can try to divert our talks with the Russians away from things that destroy man to things that will help him live a fuller life. Even though Russia feels that it is necessary to have enemies to maintain power over its people and has depicted us as the biggest devil of all, we should not react in kind. Rather we should try to cool the tension by reducing the enmity attitude to one of objectivity. Eventually, there will be a loosening of the chains that bind the people in this highly controlled state. With this greater freedom for the people, there will be greater interest on the part of the rulers to join the Alternative aligned nations; for as the voice of the people increases, the trend toward war decreases.

Except for Vietnam, which was to aid a treaty ally under attack by a totalitarian dictatorship, I can't think of a democracy that has initiated a war against another nation. All other wars that have occurred in my lifetime have been initiated by dictators and totalitarian states. If all nations had democratic governments, I doubt if international war would be much of a problem. I don't think that eliminating nuclear weapons would be a problem. This may be carrying it a bit too far, but it does tell us something. It tells us that wars are not initiated by nations where the people have control, but rather by nations where the control is in the hands of leaders who have silenced the voice of the people. In the final analysis, there are only two kinds of governments: slave and free. Free people want others to be free. Despotic rulers want all people to be slaves.

Today we live in a lawless world. This condition cannot long exist. Lawlessness, because it permits the worst in men to flourish, has always had to yield to law. Presently we are standing before the judge of time and history, trying to make up our minds whether to yield our offensive weapons to international law and enforcement or to let international war make the decision for us. Law is man's only realistic hope for a safe, healthy world society. The ultimate goal of the Alternative World Plan is effective international law with authority over all weapons classified by the Alternative Agency as offensive. The only truly offensive weapons existing in the world would be those under the control of the Alternative Enforcement Agency.

Let us not deceive ourselves by putting faith in treaties; for in a lawless world, treaties are just another form of war. A common practice among nations has been to use negotiations and treaties to hide their real intentions. Increased negotiations have often been the prelude to war. In every case during the last World War, the aggressor nations used negotiations and treaties to anesthetize their intended victims before launching military attacks. Even the wary Stalin was taken in by Hitler with this soothing tactic; so much so that, although he was told by the British and others that Hitler was planning an invasion of Russia, Stalin did not believe it until it happened.

Lenin still rules Russia, and regardless of what they say, the Russians will continue to follow Lenin almost to the letter. Why shouldn't they? Where can you find in recent centuries a philosopher whose doctrine has been spread more widely?

In 1921, Lenin wrote a memorandum that reads as follows:

"They (the capitalist nations) will supply us with the materials and the technology which we lack, and will restore our military industry which we need for our future attacks upon our suppliers. In other words, they will work hard in order to prepare their suicide.''

Lenin also said that the capitalist nations would sell Russia the rope which the Russians will use to hang the capitalist nations. In simple terms, the Alternative Defense Plan proposes to quit selling rope to hang us. With the help of the rope that the Western nations have provided them, they have built the largest military machine on earth. They have used it effectively to subjugate other nations, increase their sphere of political military influence and have forced the United States and other nations to spend untold billions on defense.

If the United States has the courage to take a firm stand on not selling rope (manufactured goods) to nations guilty of aggression or those supporting such nations, it can put the brakes on and eventually stop aggression. By courage, I mean standing solidly for freedom, having self-discipline and being willing to take a minor calculated risk. I say minor risk because

I think that under the Alternative Defense Plan the likelihood of war will be greatly reduced from what it is under our present arms course, for there will be in place a plan that focuses on a mutually beneficial goal rather than on arms. What is talked about, increases. If we actually wish to reduce arms, we must talk less about them and more about things that improve the quality of all life on earth. Action will follow the course of thought.

Russia has the same choice as every other nation. If it chooses aggression, it should pay the cost. Should it choose nonaggression and join the Alternative, agreeing to its terms, there would be no prohibition of trade in manufactured goods. It's entirely up to her. But it's also up to us. If we are opposed to aggression and see it as the mother of war, then we shouldn't support it in any way.

If Russia thinks that retaining nuclear weapons and fostering armed aggression is more important to her than protection from these weapons and unrestricted trade relations with the free industrialized nations, she will be making it clear to all nations that she prefers war to disarmament. Her words about peace and disarmament, which she has used effectively in her propaganda, will have a hollow ring; for there will be no truth in them. But she is an artist at making lies appear to be the truth and vice versa, so it will be up to the democracies to let people know the truth.

I think it is premature here to talk about specifics concerning the way the Alternative World Agency should be organized. I can, however, express my ideas in a general way. I believe that there should be a parliament of the Alternative World aligned nations. I would recommend dividing the nations into four different categories; I don't think it would be necessary for the very small nations to have a delegate, unless they thought it necessary. One delegate would be enough for nations classified as small, two delegates for nations classified as medium, and three delegates for nations classified as large. There would be no extra-large classification. The basis for rating should be a combination of population and the amount of international trade conducted. Giving them equal weight would not be a bad idea. Nations such as China and India, for example, would be classified as large despite their modest international trade. And it's possible that a nation like Japan would be given a large rating because of the very large amount of her international business. To avoid entrenchment, delegates should be elected for three or four years, and this should be on a staggered basis so that each year most of the delegates present in the parliament will have had previous experience.

I favor a relatively small governing board, perhaps as few as twenty or thirty members, all from different nations, selected by the delegates of the parliament, whose term of office would be limited and staggered as in the parliament. The board, as with many organizations, would hire the manager, the assistant manager, the secretary, and treasurer. The term of office of these job categories could be three years. The board's powers would be limited by the Articles of Incorporation of the Agency, which could be changed only by a two-thirds majority vote of the delegates. The two-thirds majority rule provides all nations protection against a group of nations, even a simple majority, from changing the terms of the Alternative. If two-thirds of the delegates voted in favor of a change, it would likely be one that is needed. The governing board would also be responsible for employing auditing firms. It would be a good idea to always have at least two auditing firms, so that one may check against the other. Their term of service should also be limited in a manner similar to the delegates and the governing board.

The thinking behind these ideas is to keep the organization as free as possible from political influence, graft, and favoritism. Having the greatest responsibility of any organization in the world, it should set an example for all nations in conducting its affairs openly and honestly.

In establishing the Alternative World Agency, there probably would be some advantage, initially, in having its headquarters in New York close to the United Nations. After its precepts become world law, it might decide to have headquarters on its own land, possibly an island or islands from which it could command its space satellites, naval and air forces. It would need command posts for its international police and accompanying arms arsenal at different strategic points around the world.

Using the same basis for financial support of the Alternative Agency (a combination of population and the amount of international trade), I think, would be fair. Any nation not having the money to pay its dues would have to borrow from other nations or the World Bank; for if it became delinquent, it would suffer severe trade sanctions. The cost of operating the Agency, compared to what nations are now paying for protection, would be so small that any nation could finance it without difficulty, particularly if the greater proportion of dues were determined by the amount of international trade.

Summarizing ADP strategy, it proposes that the United States and other free industrialized nations use their most powerful weapon, their economic power, to persuade the aggressor nations to cooperate with them in establishing an enforceable international law under which both can exist, free of the threat of annihilation by mass life-exterminating weapons. I think that Russia is sufficiently interested in this protection and in freer access to Western technology to eventually act favorably upon this proposal, assuming we and other free industrialized nations act prudently.

The time is ripe for initiating such a plan. The American economy is strong; the governments of Western Europe and most of the governments of the Western Hemisphere and the Far Eastern nations are now in the hands of democratic governments. China is opening its doors to the West. India is moving toward a freer entrepreneural society. The world is changing. Communism has had its successes, but so has democracy. The decision as to which way the world will go, slave or free government, will not be made by the totalitarian nations. This is because they can only succeed if and where democracy fails. The questions for us and every democracy is — do we have the courage to stand up for what we believe? Are we anxious and excited about challenging the future to work for us and all mankind, even the Russian people?

Challenge, Pathway To The Future

VI

Challenge, Pathway to the Future

That day in September, 1979, riding in a bus in England, I knew that I saw a light at the end of what for me had been a long dark tunnel. For over five years now, I have been groping my way toward that light. I know from experience, others can stand exactly where you are standing and not see what you see, even when you point it out to them. Is it that we see only what we are prepared to see, or is it that we see what we want to see? This question has bothered me a lot because, when others about me didn't see what I did, it has caused me to question my sight, even my sanity, to become plagued with doubt, and discouraged to the point of wanting to quit groping for this light which I thought I saw but others didn't. To explain, I quote Dr. Kenneth Boulding of the University of Colorado from a personal letter to me dated January 7, 1981, "The great problem with disarmament is the difficulty of finding a path towards it."

Fortunately, Dr. Lawrence Burkholder, a man who has spent his life in working for peace, got a glimpse of this light which I saw. His experiences as theologian, Harvard professor, and college president are very different from mine, but we had one thing in common: we were both looking for the star of hope that would lead us to the house of disarmament and peaceful coexistence. His support, his calling me every few weeks for years to ask how I was getting along with my project, made it impossible for me to quit. I don't want to imply that Dr. Burkholder and I always agreed, for often we didn't, but there was never any disagreement about our ultimate goal. I was again being challenged as I was when I started my business and when I was working on a new design for a mechanical product. Each time there was a period when I felt as I imagine Columbus did, when all about me, except a few, wanted me to abandon my search for what, to them, appeared unattainable and to return to known ground. "What was it," I have asked myself at these times, "that keeps me going when no promise of success was in sight?" In a previous chapter, I stated that the reason state-controlled enterprise could never compete successfully with free enterprise could be summed up in one word — competition. Looking back at the different ventures I cited, both of which proved to be a success, I believe that the element most responsible for these successes could also be summed up in one word — challenge. But challenge is not just a personal thing. Nations are also challenged.

Great men throughout history have challenged their generation. William Shakespeare wrote, "To be or not to be; that is the question." Every person, every nation answers to this challenge, either through action or failing to act. Those who fail to act have to accept the status imposed on them by those who act. "To be" means all of the things that Shakespeare meant, but today it has special significance for people living in free nations. They are being challenged by an adversary for the right to be free, even the right to live.

Arnold Toynbee in *The Outline of History* points out the part that challenge plays in the rise and fall of nations. The challenge that we have presented to Russia in the last fifty years, particularly the years since World War II, I believe, had a lot to do with her rise to a great world power and the creation of her mammoth war machine. The Alternative Defense Plan is designed to change the character of this challenge by ceasing the manufacture of offensive weaponry, converting the challenge from things military to things economic. Now is the time for the United States to issue this challenge for change and, should it do so, other free nations will be attracted to the same course of action.

Today the United States is the most challenged nation in the world. It is not only challenged militarily and politically by Russia, but it is also challenged by many nations in international commerce. Japan, an adversary in the last world war, through her economic capability is challenging our position in world trade. Other democracies are also being severely challenged politically and economically.

The question is, "Will the United States and other free industrialized nations rise to challenge totalitarianism's threat to freedom and life with imagination and new ideas?" Will we accept President Kennedy's challenge, "And so, my fellow Americans, ask not what your country can do for you, ask what you can do for your country." Will we challenge our people to greater individual effort in economics and other areas, thereby setting examples for other nations for exploiting the wealth of their human resources? Or will we copy the static individual-deprecating society of the socialistic state? Truly democratic society is an exciting challenge for its people because of the tremendous possibilities it offers. A socialistic society offers very little excitement for its people and few individual possibilities.

To whom does the future belong? To the democracies or the totalitarian states? I think most will agree it will go to those who are best prepared for it.

Lenin told the Russians how to prepare for their future and they have been religiously following his advice. How are the democracies going to prepare for their future? Could it be that Lenin was wrong; that in fact an open society can better prepare itself for the future than a totalitarian society? Realistically, we know that the dead, no matter how clever in their lifetime, are not able to see the future, except in terms of what they knew and saw when they lived. Lenin saw Russia's future in terms of military power and a Communist society. But he didn't foresee the nuclear bomb, the computer, or the space age, all of which have changed the world in ways unimaginable to him and in ways that we don't yet fully appreciate. Might not the nuclear bomb which now threatens our existence be used by man to throw off the oppression of military power and open to us all the path to a new world?

If we only look at the confrontation between the United States and Russia, we could conclude that Lenin was right. The Russians have made his prophecy come true. Next to providing an adequate deterrent to Russian aggression, the first question that the democracies need to resolve in planning their future is whether they are going to think like Marx and Lenin, or like the men who founded the United States. We don't need to conjecture what the future will be like under Marx's and Lenin's thinking; Russia stands as living proof. The United States stands as proof of the value in the thinking of the men who established the United States.

Shouting from their sick bed, the Communists are still proclaiming that the next century will belong to Communism. God forbid, but they could be right. It could happen, but only if the democracies lose faith in themselves and succumb to the military threat, political propaganda and bluff of the Soviet Union. There is a lot of air in the Russian threat, but this is no immediate solace for the democracies, for the Communists have deluded themselves into believing that their socialistic economy works for the good of mankind, although they have proven that it does not. It works very well for a few, but for the majority it has meant scarcity and slavery. There is probably no nation in the world today where the caste system is as great and as solidly entrenched as it is in Russia.

Interestingly, it was Karl Marx, the man best known for his ideas for a classless, Communist society (a workman's paradise free from class oppression), who fathered the existing Russian society. Had he possessed understanding as well as knowledge, he might not have become so self-enamored with his idealistic ideas as to become blind to the realities of human nature. But overcome with an obsession that the bourgeoisie were the real cause of the working people's plight, his thinking was frozen in a warped position which prevented him from making deeper inquiry. Foolishly he thought that the proletariat was more benign and, if in a position of power, would create a Communist workingman's paradise free from class oppression. Today we can see that the hole in Marxist thinking, rather than liberating the workingman, has put him under oppression equivalent to slavery. Although there were others of similar thinking, it's my belief that it was Marx's emotional manifesto of his impractical theories that have placed Russia in the position that she is today and is the root cause of our confrontation with Russia. Had Marx heeded the admonition of King Solomon about gaining knowledge, that above all gain understanding, the world might be a different place than it is today.

In challenging totalitarianism, democracies need to remember that their hope for and picture of the future is quite different from that of the Communists. Democracies, as a whole, see the future as an expanding economy through entrepreneurship, science, and development of human resources. In contrast to this, the Communists' hope rests on their ability to subdue the democracies to make their dream come true. Quite a challenge! Probably the greatest challenge the democracies have ever faced. Are they up to it? That is the question. They stand at the threshhold of a new world created through their science. But do they see themselves as the wave of the future, or is their face turned toward socialism? If this is true, then the question of whether the democracies are to survive and prevail may already be answered. For it is in a rebirth of democracy that they can best find their strength for fashioning their future. Free enterprise is still the greatest source of wealth for a nation. Socialism, rather than creating wealth, distributes scarcity, because the basis for its distribution is political rather than production.

What is the best way for the democracies to challenge totalitarianism? It is unwise to discount the Russian military threat. But overreacting is also unwise, as it might cause the Samson of armament to bring down the temple of humanity on himself and the rest of the world. Therefore, the challenge must allow Russia to keep things that she considers vital to her existence (providing, of course, that these are not threats to our existence) and to exchange things that are not vital for things of much greater value.

Put yourself in Russia's shoes for a moment. Is it likely that she considers armed aggression more important to her success than trade on manufactured goods with the democracies? I think not, for she can promote her ideology in other ways, as she possesses the world's greatest propaganda machine. While not admitting it, she probably envies the productivity of free enterprise because her system of complete state control has produced an economic morass from which she seems unable to extricate herself. Lenin taught there is no situation from which you cannot extricate yourself and, when he saw that Communism was not working, he turned to world conquest as a way out. If Lenin were alive today, would he still say that political power flows from military power?

Still standing in Russia's shoes, we face a real dilemma. Our world political position rests primarily on our military power; if we cannot use it or it becomes less of a threat, will this not erode our position as a superpower? We know that some of our satellites are increasing their productivity by loosening state controls. And, when we look to the east and south, we see China doing the same thing with similar results. The prospect is unsettling for us Russians. China could become more powerful than we, and our satellites might prefer her Communism to ours. We realize that a loosening of state control of the economy, eventually, is almost inevitable, but if we allow more economic freedom, won't this also create a demand for more personal freedom? We can't take our problems to China; that would be humiliating. To take them to the nations of Western Europe, unless of course we could completely control them, would mean losing face because we must maintain a position of apparent supremacy over them. The United States, our rival, has given us just about everything that we have wanted. It's far enough away so that we don't have any border problems. Secretly we admire their ingenuity. Since nuclear war seems out of the question and there seems to be a resurgence of patriotism in the United States, we have to put off bringing them under our control for a while. In the meantime, why not strengthen our economic relationship with the United States? They can help us resolve our economic problem. This will keep China and our satellites in their places or, at least, not allow them to surpass us in technology and modern production methods.

To some, this little scenario may seem far-fetched. But I believe that the pragmatists in the Kremlin, for the short term, would be happy to soft pedal aggression in exchange for closer economic ties with the United States, for there are cracks developing in her armor and her Achilles heel is now well exposed. The problem with this is that the Communist Russian government needs enemies to justify its enormous expenditures for their military and the lack of consumer goods for their people. We have been obliging Russia by reacting in normal enemy fashion without using the ingenuity for which she gives us credit. To have this enemy relationship dissolve into a friendship relationship would create serious problems for the Kremlin rulers. Their people might find out that their government hasn't always been telling them the truth; on the contrary, it has been giving them a lot of misinformation. I believe that an enemy relationship is probably the only relationship available with Russia and is not necessarily a bad relationship, if we accept it as a matter of fact and learn to live with it and deal with it, at least for the foreseeable future. How we get along with the Russians depends more upon our conduct than it does on theirs. If we jump every time the Russian bear growls and go into an orgy of criticizing ourselves, they will never respect us. Respect is the most important ingredient in our relationship with Russia. We can have it, if we answer the bear's growls with truth, quietly but firmly, and in a way that others can see the lies and misinformation in his statements.

Most Americans have little understanding of the economic powerhouse called the United States of

America. Its products are sold in practically every nation of the world and most of them are considered the standard of the world. Its dollar is the world's common currency. Of whom should we be afraid? Why do we say we are afraid of the Russians? The prevalent answer is because of their excessive armament or their Communistic ideology, but is this really the whole truth? Could it be that much of our fear is founded on ignorance, emotion, prejudice, an unwillingness to face reality, and, most important of all, lack of self-confidence?

When we face reality, make careful evaluation and put things in proper perspective, we come up with an entirely different picture of the possibilities that are open to us in resolving the Russian confrontation. For then we can clearly see ourselves as we are. We can compare our strengths and our weaknesses with the strengths and weaknesses of the Russians. At present most Americans have a prejudiced and emotional view towards the Russians; some think they are supermen; others think they are subhumans devoid of reason and

compassion. Americans need to rise above the petti-
ness of blame, accusations, counting weapons, etc.
and concentrate on what is important, which is long-
term coexistence with the Russians in a way that removes the fear of mass life-threatening weapons. Some
have called this idealistic dreaming, forgetting or not
knowing that dreams are the substance from which
things are made. The fearful, the negative thinkers,
say it will not work, but it has always been so until
somebody or some people make it work.

"Consider nothing impossible before it has come
to pass." – Confucius

Many think that we can talk ourselves out of the
nuclear arms problem. To me, this is trying to escape
our responsibility and not facing the reality that the
Frankenstein monster we created has grown up and
possesses a power of its own. It will still submit to
man's authority because what man has made he can
destroy, but he cannot dissolve a monster as large as

nuclear armament with words alone, even if he talked continuously for a thousand days. To solve a problem as large and well established as nuclear armament requires much more than words. It was created by imagination, skill and physical power and such will be required to remove it.

In summary, I would like to say again that I think Emerson was right in thinking of reality as the supreme good. Are there any among us who believe that individual nations can be trusted with nuclear weapons, who believe that man has outgrown his murderous ways, his unfeeling attitude for people of other nations, and is now so godlike that he would not use the most murderous weapon to destroy his enemies? I think we know the answer to this question. But we have not yet faced up to the reality that, if our nation doesn't take the responsibility for the action needed to eliminate nuclear weapons in the hands of individual nations, nuclear war is inevitable. Under the Alternative Defense Plan, nuclear war is avoidable.

Like you, I am only one person, but you too probably have relatives in the family in which you were born, also a spouse, perhaps children, maybe even grandchildren. My life will come to an end; it's just a matter of years. Why then should I be so concerned? Is death not the lot of all? I've had people say that to me. The thought that there are people who think that way, rather than discouraging me, has caused me to increase my effort to let more people know that there is a way, a practical feasible way, of avoiding a nuclear hell, of turning MAD (Mutual Assured Destruction) into MAS (Mutual Assured Survival).

Writing this book has brought me to the realization that *our greatest enemy is not Russia. It is our apathy in dealing with reality.*

I believe that now is the time to reevaluate the economic strength of democracy and free enterprise. It is time for a rebirth of commitment to the ideal of preserving our planet free from nuclear bondage or destruction. Ours is the generation that can launch the legacy of an Alternative World of peace and opportunity. You can be a part of this new world.

*"The only thing necessary for evil to triumph
is for good men to do nothing."*
— *Edmond Burke*

WE AMERICANS

AS THE NATION THAT BROUGHT TO OUR
EARTH THE NUCLEAR PLAGUE THAT NOW
THREATENS THE LIFE AND HOPES OF ALL
LIVING PERSONS, THE QUESTION THAT WE
AMERICANS NEED TO ASK OURSELVES
IS—

WHAT KIND OF PEOPLE ARE WE? ARE
WE IRRESPONSIBLE, UNCARING FOR
THE LIVES OF OTHERS, SO FAITHLESS
THAT WE CANNOT MUSTER THE WILL
TO MAKE THE SUPREME EFFORT TO
DO WHAT WE CAN AND KNOW MUST
BE DONE?

*WE NEED TO FIND THE COURAGE TO DO
THE RIGHT THING, TO PAY THE DEBT WE
OWE, TO GIVE BACK TO THE PEOPLE OF
OUR EARTH A WORLD FREE OF NUCLEAR
WEAPONS.*

All publishing rights assigned to

ALTERNATIVE WORLD FOUNDATION, INC.
803 North Main Street
Goshen, Indiana 46526
(219) 534-3402